THIS BOOK I...

....

THE WORLD'S MOST CHARMING/
OFFENSIVE/KISSABLE/PATHETIC/
FOUL/UGLY/BEAUTIFUL/TAUREAN

WITH KIND REGARDS/DROP DEAD/
LOVE AND KISSES...................

P.S. PLEASE TAKE NOTE OF PAGE(S)

....

THE TAURUS BOOK

A CORGI BOOK 0 552 12317 X

First publication in Great Britain
PRINTING HISTORY
Corgi edition published 1983

Copyright © Ian Heath 1983

Corgi Books are published by Transworld Publishers Ltd.,
Century House, 61-63 Uxbridge Road, Ealing, London W5 5SA

Made and printed in Great Britain by the
Guernsey Press Co. Ltd., Guernsey, Channel Islands.

THE TAURUS BOOK

BY IAN HEATH

TAURUS

APRIL 21 – MAY 20

SECOND SIGN OF THE ZODIAC
SYMBOL: THE BULL
RULING PLANET: VENUS
COLOURS: DEEP ROSE, DEEP BLUE
GEMS: TURQUOISE, SAPPHIRE
NUMBER: SIX
DAY: FRIDAY
METAL: COPPER
FLOWER: FORGET-ME-NOT

The TAUREAN at work...............

ZZZZZZZZZZ

...FRIENDLY TO CO-WORKERS.....

.........NEVER SHOUTS..........

> WELL ER, UM MAYBE
> NO I DON'T THINK SO
> YES ER MAYBE
> NICE WEATHER FOR
> THE TIME OF YEAR
> UM NOT SURE
> RING ME LATER
> YES NO YES OH I
> DUNNO 'BYE

.... IS DECISIVE ....

.... CREATIVE ....

....CAN GET IN A RUT..........

...... ARRIVES EARLY ....

.... PLUMBER..................

.........CHIROPODIST................

...... OR ROAD-SWEEPER.

.....ENJOYS ROMANTIC MUSIC........

.... WALLPAPERING ....

.... IS INTO D.I.Y. ....

...... KEEPS ANIMALS ....

..... ADORES GARDENING ....

.......LIKES TO RELAX...........

.... IS SUPPORTIVE...........

.... AND IS HOUSE-PROUD.

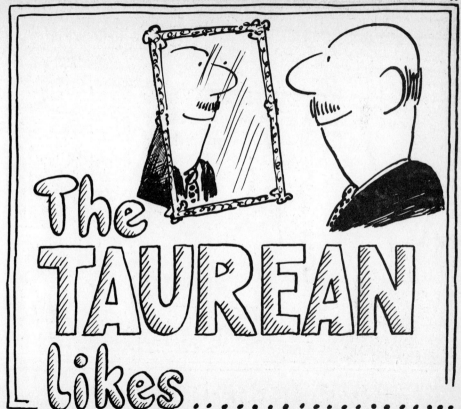

...... SMART CLOTHES ....

..........SKIING...................

.... CAMPING ....

.... AND BOILED EGGS.

.... DANDRUFF ....

......CRYSTALLIZED FRUIT..........

.... AND BEING ILL.

The TAUREAN in love...............

.... IS JEALOUS ....

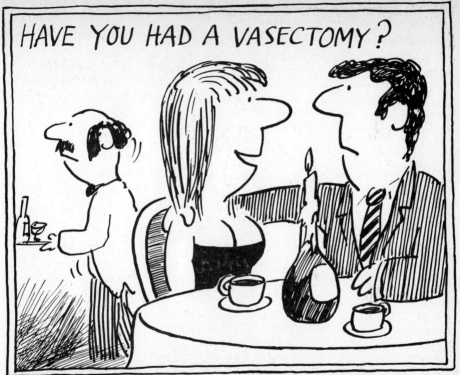

.... SINCERE ....

.... CALCULATING ....

.... FAITHFUL ....

.... DEMANDING ....

> YOU'RE GENEROUS, VERY INTELLIGENT, HANDSOME, ATHLETIC, GREAT FUN, AWARE, GOOD IN BED, BEAUTIFUL, HARD-WORKING, KIND, MATURE, VERY LOVING, ARTISTIC, KIND, UNDERSTANDING, GENTLE, ETC, ETC., ETC., ETC.,

> IS THAT ALL?

...ENJOYS BEING FLATTERED........

...AND LIKES THE LIGHTS OUT.

TAUREAN AND PARTNER

HEART RATINGS

♥♥♥♥♥ WOWEE!!
♥♥♥♥ GREAT, BUT NOT 'IT'
♥♥♥ O.K. — COULD BE FUN
♥♥ FORGET IT
♥ WALK QUICKLY THE OTHER WAY

VIRGO CAPRICORN

GEMINI CANCER PISCES
ARIES

AQUARIUS LEO TAURUS

SCORPIO

LIBRA SAGITTARIUS

TAURUS PEOPLE

ELLA FITZGERALD: SOCRATES
BING CROSBY: AUDREY HEPBURN
LEONARDO DA VINCI
TCHAIKOVSKY: ORSON WELLES
WILLIAM RANDOLPH HEARST

H. M. QUEEN ELIZABETH II
FRED ASTAIRE: LIBERACE
ROBERT BROWNING: GARY COOPER
HITLER: JAMES M. BARRIE
MARGOT FONTEYN: HENRY FONDA
WILLIAM SHAKESPEARE
HO CHI MINH: SHIRLEY MacLAINE
SALVADOR DALI: KARL MARX
LENIN: RUDOLPH VALENTINO
ANTHONY QUINN: JOE LOUIS
BRAHMS: OLIVER CROMWELL